If You Want
a Job Done Right

Hire a Woman

If You Want a Job Done Right

Hire a Woman

Michael Williams
with Paris Williams

TATE PUBLISHING
AND ENTERPRISES, LLC

Published by Tate Publishing & Enterprises, LLC
127 E. Trade Center Terrace | Mustang, Oklahoma 73064 USA
1.888.361.9473 | www.tatepublishing.com

Tate Publishing is committed to excellence in the publishing industry. The company reflects the philosophy established by the founders, based on Psalm 68:11,
"The Lord gave the word and great was the company of those who published it."

Book design copyright © 2014 by Tate Publishing, LLC. All rights reserved.

Published in the United States of America

ISBN: 978-1-63122-894-0
1. Self-Help / Fashion & Style
2. Education / Counseling / Career Guidance
14.01.22

Contents

Introduction

Whether you are 16 and seeking your first part-time job while still in high school; getting ready to graduate from college and launch your first career; or a seasoned veteran of the business world looking to begin a second, third, or fourth career, the advice in these chapters on approaching the business and career world will help you with:

- Researching your options

- Dressing for success

- Preparing for an interview

- Following through to land a job

Women everywhere, every day, show the world the truth of the title: *If You Want a Job Done Right, Hire a Woman*

Researching various companies to find the one that is right for you will keep you from wasting time on companies, businesses, school districts, or any potential employer whose work climate does not fit your individual needs. Having a sense of accomplishment and job satisfaction are just as important as the amount of money you earn.

Once you've found one or more companies you think are right for you, dressing and acting in positive ways and being prepared for an interview will go a long way toward helping you land that perfect job.

The practical tips all through this book will help you become the best woman you can be.

Chapter 1 :

Research Companies
to Find a Good Match

Do you have a best friend? I mean a true best friend, someone whom you like and trust, and vice versa? That is how you should feel about the company you work for. The effort you put into researching companies to find one that fits your needs and appreciates what you do will pay off, not only in terms of money, but also in personal satisfaction. So keep looking for a company that will be a good match for your skills and one where you feel you will fit into the company culture.

To take an example from the writing world, a good author researches markets before sending out a manuscript. It would be a waste of time and resources to send an action/adventure novel to a company that publishes romances. Nor would a person send a children's book manuscript to a company listing only erotica. These are extremes, but if you hate to fly, applying to an international company that advertises the fact that it sends employees traveling would be equally ridiculous.

There are several places you can research a company. The amount of time you have will determine what source you use. The Internet is the fastest source. Library sources might include Dun and Bradstreet lists of companies as well as Standard & Poor's Register. These lists store a wealth of information about companies. If time allows, you might ask the company you are interested in for information about themselves.

Mentors can also be helpful. If you are seeking employment in a certain field, it would be advisable to find someone who works in that field and ask them for help and suggestions. Mentors can guide you with interview preparation and with choosing career paths. You can find out what is expected from you if you seek one type of job or another. A mentor can also point out the pitfalls of being in a certain field, the high points, advantages or disadvantages of a particular position, and so on.

If you cannot find a mentor, try to network with people in your chosen industry or company. In time you will meet someone who can direct you.

What different criteria can be used to determine a good match? In other words, what would be an easy definition for the term "Dream Job"?

A Dream Job might be defined as employment that one enjoys doing. It provides a challenge and purpose, and a feeling of accomplishment when it allows a person to reach his or her financial goals. I have heard it said, to the point where it is becoming a cliché, "Find something that you enjoy doing for a living, and you will never have to work. Still, it is true.

Here are a few examples of women who found their true callings by various means:

1. I heard a story about a woman who enjoys her job so much it brings tears to her eyes each day. Her name is Suzy and she is a Registered Nurse at

one of the leading hospitals in her state. She is well known and everyone in the nursing circles in the city respects her. The mayor of the city has recognized her as a leading citizen in the community. Suzy says she loves her job because she is in love with her purpose of saving lives and helping people get through times of illness. Yes, she has seen death, and she realizes that some days are a challenge, with no rainbow at the end of the day. But she still feels she has the best job in the world. You see, Suzy has a secret that has been hidden from everyone for years—a second job that is intertwined with her main job. Suzy's secret is that she is a clown on the children's floor in the hospital where she works. Nobody has ever been able to see through her disguise. Suzy says that the smiles she sees on the children's faces keep her coming back for more. And though there are some rainy days in her job, there are many more sunny days. Suzy has found her passion and purpose, and you will find yours the day you find your dream job.

2. A kindergarten teacher I met in Houston, Texas, always had her students draw a picture of themselves during the first week of school. She kept these pictures in a file. As the year went along, she added to each child's collection, always dating each picture or work sample. At the end of the year, tired and ready to send those kids home to their parents for the summer, she would go through the files and look at the huge amount of progress each child had made during the year. Sometimes tears came to her eyes as she stapled each child's collection so it was ready to give back to them and their parents as a memento of that year in school. "What in the world are you doing?" her husband asked one year. "Seeing my

reason to go back next August," she said. "When I see how far they've come, how much they've learned, it makes the whining, hitting, temper tantrums, struggling to learn, and all the other day-to-day frustrations worth it." This teacher knew teaching was her vocation, her true calling, in spite of the frustrations that often came with the job.

3. Two sisters attended the same university. Both decided to major in accounting. But once they graduated, their careers took very different paths. The older of the two was an extrovert and loved being around lots of people. She liked the high stress and competition of larger corporations. Once she had the years of experience necessary and had passed the CPA exam, she focused her career on moving up in the corporate world and into the area of internal audit. Her ultimate goal was to become a consultant. She viewed each company she worked for as a place to learn additional skills, find new challenges, and increase her marketability. By her late thirties, she was earning six figures and was ready to launch her own consulting firm. The younger sister was less outgoing. She was not shy, but knew that the career path her sister had chosen was not for her. She applied to smaller companies and found herself at home with an accounting firm whose clients were small businesses. She excelled in preparing quarterly statements, payroll records, and other traditional accounting services. From there she moved up into tax work for her firm. The older sister, who hates doing tax work, refers clients to her younger sister for their tax work. These two young women are both happy in their jobs and neither would want to trade places. Each one thought about her own personality type and

what made her happy when applying for jobs. Even though they do not earn similar salaries, both are content.

4. Sometimes women fall into careers or businesses quite by accident. The Amilya Antonetti story is a clear example of this. Amilya, a married working mom, had everything a woman could dream of. When she brought her newborn son home from the hospital, panic was in the air. The baby could not breathe and ugly rashes began to show on his skin. So she did what any mother would do. She took him to the emergency room. One doctor told her that the problem was in her mind. Another doctor told her to let this one go, meaning let her child die, that there was no help for him.

Another person from whom she sought help told her to keep a diary of everything she was doing at home. This suggestion upset Amilya. She already had too many things on her plate! Reluctantly, she followed the advice. She noticed that David, her son, always became ill on Tuesdays and off to the hospital they went.

But what was so special about Tuesdays? Tuesdays were the days she did a thorough house-cleaning. That was when she discovered that the household products she was using were killing her son.

Now what? She called the woman who hung the sun every day, her grandma, for advice. She flew her grandma in for a visit, for some help. Grandma's remedy was natural cleaners... cleaners without harsh chemicals. This was the experience that changed not only Amilya's life, but also the lives of thousands of others.

After this discovery, Amilya was filled with relief, but she was bursting with the question, "Who else? Who else could be suffering like David?" She put a small ad in the local penny paper, inviting moms to come to a meeting if they had similar problems. Amilya was expecting only a handful at most. Over 200 moms showed up!

That meeting was the beginning of Soapworks.

Amilya admits it was not easy by any measure. But she stayed true to her mission, despite all the distractions that came along. She was a strong-willed person who would go to any lengths to save her children.

Amilya knew she had a good idea that was needed by the world if she could only find the right help. She knew no one could bring off this great accomplishment alone. She knocked on many doors trying to find a chain that would carry her products. When knocking on doors didn't work, she sneaked into a plant whose CEO she had been trying to speak with for eight months. This CEO's first name was Bob. Once inside the plant, she stood in the hallway asking every man if he was Bob. When a man finally answered that he was Bob, she asked, "Bob, can I get those three minutes of your time that I have been trying to get for the last eight months?" Three minutes were granted, and the subsequent sale was over a million dollars.

Amilya has been on Oprah, CNN, and Fox, and many articles have been written about her success. People want to know how she went from making products to protect her son to a multimillion-dollar business. You can read more about her story at Amilya.com.

The stories presented here are only a few of thousands, or perhaps millions, of possibilities. Now, let's take a look at your own life, your skills, dreams, and passions to see where you might fit in best with a career or a company.

What is in your Dynamic Natural Ability, your DNA? What were you meant to do for the rest of your life?

Wouldn't it be a perfect world if everyone could figure out why they were put here on earth? If everyone could know what their best ability was so they could be the best they could be? And not only that, they would probably love what they did for a living. Some people are just that fortunate—they've figured out their job DNA with respect to what they are best able to do. It is their Dynamic Natural Ability. Here are a few striking examples of women and their DNA at work:

Barbara Walters	News Reporter
Oprah Winfrey	TV Host
Pat Willard	High School Teacher
Dana Kilpatrick	Race Car Driver
Suzy Jones	Registered Nurse/Clown
Beth Sanchez	Teacher
Hillary Clinton	Politician
Erica Sorenson	Pro Golfer
Cindy Williams	Salesperson

The list could go on forever.

Sadly, there are many more people who work for years and years at jobs they hate. So, the question is: what is your job DNA?

Let us take a hypothetical idea as a test to try to figure your DNA for a job or career analysis. If a billionaire were to offer you money each year (say, a million dollars or more) to do anything on earth you choose to do, what would you really have a passion to do for the next 30 years? Remember, you will not be working for money because you will get more than you would need to spend in a lifetime. Granted, this is not a real-world situation, but job satisfaction is just as important as the amount of money you make.

One way to begin to find your DNA is to ask yourself a few questions. The answers may give you a better insight as to whether a particular job will match your DNA. These are also good questions to ask yourself before any interview:

1. What skills do you have, or want to develop, to make you suited for this job?

2. Why do you want this job?

3. Are your skills really compatible with this company and the services they provide?

4. Can you see your future with this company regardless of the position?

5. What do you know about this company?

Besides the company's location, try to learn as much as possible about the company so you are knowledgeable about the products and services they provide, the number of years they have been in business, their locations around the city or world, their higher-ranking officers' names, their customer targets, their competition, and anything else you deem vital to your getting hired by the right company.

Now, let us discuss some parameters you might want to use to figure out what makes you tick.

1. Who would be your ideal work partners?

a. Do you like working alone, with a few people, or with many people?

b. Do you like working with children, teens, your age group, older, or elderly?

c. Do you like working with all races and nationalities, or do you prefer certain groups?

d. Do you like working with rich, or poor, neither, or both?

e. Do you prefer working with males or females?

f. Do you want to work with famous or well-known people?

g. Maybe you prefer to work with animals, or nature.

2. **Environment is the next category we will use to measure your job DNA.**

   a. Do you prefer to work in a small office by yourself, or with a few (less than 25) coworkers?

   b. Do you like working in a large building with 1000+ coworkers?

   c. Would you like working for a firm that sends you to different locations all over the city, all day?

   d. Would you like traveling the world to feed your passion?

   e. Maybe you are an outdoors person and love the beauty of nature.

3. **Ego.**

   a. Do you want a job that makes you feel like a celebrity?

   b. Do you like having authority and being a leader?

   c. Do you like working with your hands, or having an intellectual challenge?

   d. Do you aspire to be your own boss, or head the company?

4. **Time of the day.**

   a. Are you a morning person who prefers an 8-to-5 schedule?

   b. Are you a person who likes to work the night shift?

c. Does the shift matter?

d. Do you want to work weekends or not?

Some people make millions of dollars working a few hours a week, but hate what they do. What you do for a living has some effect on your everyday happiness. Happiness has an effect on longevity. Unhappiness and stress often lead to burnout, depression, and physical illness. These can be signals that a career change is in order.

The teacher mentioned above discovered another passion during her teaching career—writing. Trying to do both was so stressful that she suffered a "stress attack" one day at school. An ambulance trip to a hospital (her principal thought she may have had a heart attack) and the days of rest that followed made her realize it was time to choose between the two competing passions. She retired from teaching at the end of that school year. She now balances a little substitute teaching with long days of writing and has not been sick a single day since she left the full-time job in the classroom.

I am sure there are other parameters that can be used to discover your job DNA. Finding your Dream Job sometimes takes a stroke of luck. If you know what your passion and purpose are, finding your DNA will be a cinch. Find your passion and purpose, plan it, and just do it.

Doing research on different companies can be vital to landing your Dream Job. You might be right for a company, but is the company right for you? The best time to start researching a company would be now. Do not wait until the last minute if at all possible.

If you are in college and you know what industry and major you want to study, start researching companies by following their progress while you are in school. Do an internship with one or more companies if possible. Or do some volunteer work in an area you think might be right for you. By the time you begin to interview, you will probably know more about the company than the person interviewing you, which should be a plus for you.

Try to learn about the company's products or the services they provide. Know their competition. Follow their profits and losses. Know the structure and staff of the company, and also of its subsidies. The more you know, the better able you will be to find a company that is as good a fit as possible for your Dream Job.

If possible, find out a company's turnover rate. If people stay only a year or two on average, it says something about what it might be like to work there. If people tend to stay until they retire, that says something, too.

What is a company looking for in the person they want to hire? To answer this, ask yourself the following questions because they are the questions corporations ask themselves when they are trying to recruit the perfect employee.

Am I going to be an asset or a liability to the company?
Am I a team player?
Do I have the right attitude to fit in this company's culture?
Do I look and dress like I can represent this company in a positive manner?
Can I stay motivated to do the job?

Companies want a person who can increase their bottom line and polish their public image. Candidates who are hired usually bring some talent or skill to their employer The risk a company takes is whether the candidate will be worth the investment the company will be making in training, company benefits, image building, salary, and so forth.

Webster's dictionary defines "attitude" as the manner in which you show your feelings and thoughts. Job skills are a must to do the job, but a good attitude can often be the reason a person is hired. A person can be taught to do a job, but it is very difficult to teach attitude. A company would rather have a person with no skill and a good attitude than someone with skill and a bad attitude. Candidates with good attitudes make better employees and are easier to direct and train in the company's way of doing things. An employee with a bad attitude will run customers to the competition.

Company image is the way a company wants to be perceived by its customers, and the public in general. The image of the company is mainly in the hands of the employees through marketing, customer service, community service, and employee efforts to represent the company by the way they dress, speak, and carry themselves in public.

Workers who are motivated can also be labeled dependable. In order for a company to stay alive in this economy, it must have motivated workers. Companies want people who do not need babysitting, and are self-motivated. The more candidates they hire who are motivated, the greater the company's chances to make a profit. Motivated employees tend to be more punctual and dependable. They are goal setters with the determination to do a good job. Dependable people make better team players and team players make a winning team. Be motivated to be a winner.

Chapter 2 :
Dressing to Land a Job

When it comes to fashion, and what to wear for a special occasion, women are more skilled than men. Women are practically born with fashion sense. Little girls are given dolls while boys get balls and guns. Girls get to play fashion designer with their dolls. They also pretend to be grown-ups as they dress in their mommies' clothes at their tea parties. When they finish with the dolls and tea parties, they graduate to their own looks. Girls' abilities evolve into the expertise of a woman and continue to grow throughout their fashion years. However, because fashion is so subjective, opinion driven, and changes like the wind, what to wear for an interview is not always clear. Whether or not to wear a suit, the hairstyle and grooming, perfume, and the amount of jewelry are just a few factors that need to be considered.

When preparing for an interview, ask yourself, "What are the first thoughts the interviewer will have about me in the initial 15 to 20 seconds?" The real question is: what do you want them to think of you in those first crucial seconds? The interviewer might wonder if you are trustworthy or if you can do the job, because companies must hire employees whom they believe to be honest and who will not steal from, or deceive, the company. Other concerns for the interviewer might be: what level of sophistication does this person have? Is this person promotable?

Companies want to hire people who will fit within the company culture. No one likes to be embarrassed and neither do companies.

Finally, an important consideration the interviewer might have is: can this candidate meet our image projections? Remember that the person hired—you—will represent the company, and a company's image is very important. Companies are looking for people who can grow with them.

Many people have creative ways of dressing. When you think about the different ways women dress, you can think of the different types there are in the industry. People usually want to express their personality through the way they dress. For example, highly fashionable women wear brand-name clothes that may be hard to find in any mall or shopping center. Calvin Klein, Versace, Gucci, and Chanel are some of the brands you would see these women wearing. They may also have exotic makeup or one feature about their face that stands out—perhaps their eyebrows, eyelashes, or lips.

We all realize that hairstyles are a personal choice. You may be the type of person who believes that your hair makes you who you are, so changing your hairstyle is unthinkable. And that is okay. But keep in mind that companies can hire whomever they please. A person who will not change a hairstyle to increase their chances of getting a job will probably not change other things for the benefit of the company.

For most, makeup for an interview will be a little different than for going out on a date or a night on the town. It is better to have too little makeup than too much. It is better to look like an intelligent librarian than a singer in a nightclub. Unless the job you are applying for is the headline singer in a nightclub…then it would be appropriate to dress that way.

Depending on the position, job interviews require a certain dress code. Not every interview requires a suit, but the better you look, the better your chance to be chosen by the company. For corporate positions, we recommend skirted suits in black, dark grey, or navy. Make sure your suit is a good fit. If your garments are too tight or your skirt is too short, the interviewer might misunderstand what you are selling. If you have to keep adjusting your skirt while seated, maybe it is too short or too tight. In some industries, pants might be considered too casual for a corporate interview. A white blouse with a high neckline is perfect. Light blue and other pastel colors also work.

In the noncorporate world, other styles or colors may be appropriate once you are on the job. For example, nurses, medical technicians, and others involved in health care generally wear various forms of "scrubs" on the job. Police officers, private security firms, etc., all have standard uniforms. Teachers of young children often wear more casual clothes, especially the "wash and wear" variety, because of the mishaps and messes that frequently occur in the classroom. But as a candidate for a job, where you might be meeting with school administrators, hospital officials, or heads of police departments, it is still best to be dressed professionally when going to an interview.

The way you accessorize your suit is very important and can indicate something about your sophistication. Too many pieces of jewelry can show a lack of class. We recommend only one earring, no bigger than the size of a nickel, in each ear. Wearing multiple earrings in each ear is a fad and some companies might view you as having a renegade personality. Lip rings, eyebrow rings, and facial jewelry are also not a good idea.

However, if you are applying to work in a boutique that sells lip rings and the like, you might want to look that part. On the other hand, if you were starting up a business of your own with such a boutique, you would most certainly not wear these items to meet the banker from whom you are seeking a small-business loan.

One necklace, such as a small pearl necklace, works. Large fashion neckwear may be considered too trendy for an executive interview. If you choose not to wear a necklace, consider a coordinating scarf. Other jewelry to wear might be a watch, a bracelet, and a ring on each hand.

Other accessories for women going on an interview might be closed-toe, one-inch heels and a matching handbag or valise, along with a coordinating belt, if needed. Let us not forget to mention hosiery. Your hose should be close to your skin tone, and should not be made of mesh or have any insignia.

Now that you are dressed for the interview, look in a full-length mirror and count your accessories. If you have more than ten, remove something. If you see any items that shine too much or are distracting, remove them. You want the interviewer to concentrate on you and what you have to say, not on your shiny jewelry. It is better to look conservative than to look like a party girl.

If possible, pay a visit beforehand to the business or company you would like to work for. Act like a visitor, or simply pretend you are lost. Take a good look around and note what the employees are wearing, to see what will be expected of you. Be sure this visit is not on "casual Friday."

What to Wear

"Classic Conservative" goes a long way in helping women find their place in most companies.

The saying goes, "When in Rome, do as the Romans do." The business world does not wear togas, nor should you. This is the perfect interview suit for the corporate world: black suit, white blouse, black pumps with matching bags/folios.

Ready for their first day on the job: (left) 2-piece suit with below-the-knee skirt and ankle-strap pumps, and (right) another 2-piece medium grey suit, and black pumps.

What <u>Not</u> to Wear

These styles are great for weekend nights out, casual times with friends, or trying to impress some young man. They might also work if your goal is to work in or own a shop that sells these items.

However, they will not impress the loan officer at a bank or a potential employer, especially if that loan officer or potential employer is a woman.

What to Wear — Shoes

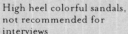

High heel colorful sandals, not recommended for interviews

Black or navy pumps are always appropriate for your corporate interview

Hosiery should be of your skin-tone without any special design embroidered

Accessories & Hair Styles

Always wear conservative jewelry… small to medium size pearls are perfect for that important interview.

Hairstyles: you be the judge… conservative is better.

Chapter 3 :

Preparing for the Interview ... Common Mistakes to Avoid

If you had a major test coming up for a class and wanted to get an A, would you neglect studying the night before? Did not practicing ever get a sports team to the championship? Of course not. Getting a job is no different. It requires study, practice, and preparation.

Preparation is one of the keys to any successful accomplishment. If you are preparing for a driving test, going on a date, or taking a vacation trip, you would prepare appropriately. Let us use the example of taking a vacation to another country. There are several preparatory tasks that would be necessary to make your vacation a successful one. You will need a passport. Your passport says something about you, just as your resume or job application does. You should check to see what the weather conditions will be so you will know what clothing to pack. You should know what the currency exchange rate will be so you have some idea how much money you should take. Preparing for interviews is very similar to preparing for any activity you are planning.

Make sure everything about you looks and sounds professional.

Your answering machine's outgoing message should be a professional one. "This is Fancy Dancer. Leave your message for this sweet girl and we'll get back to you later. Kisses." A message like this is a sure way of not getting a call back...guaranteed.

This goes for your e-mail address, too. Using sexychick@hotmail.com or other "cute" addresses won't leave the impression you want a potential employer to have.

Make sure all the e-mails or any written communication you send to a prospective company are "dressed" for the occasion. Use business-letter format, always.

If you need to leave a voice mail, make it sound as confident as the introduction you'll make when you arrive for an interview.

Resumes are like a salesman's business card. They need to be informational and very eye-catching. Resumes are used by potential employers as a quick screening device. If your resume does not have an impressive professional look, chances are you will not get an interview. Human resource personnel may have hundreds of resumes to review, and the ones that attract attention will have a better chance of getting reviewed.

Another mistake you can make is not preparing for your interview. Practice helps. Try to anticipate possible questions and prepare good answers that show how you will fill the needs of the company. Learn to relax; practice the interview process with a friend. Try to have prepared answers as to why this company should hire you. (We will review some possible questions in the next chapter.)

I recently went to a job fair at a local college and asked all of the interviewing companies if they would help me with a short survey. The survey was to help to determine why some students never get a call for an interview. The first question on the survey was:

What disturbs you the most about candidates?

The top four answers were:

- Poor appearance
- Lack of interest
- Lack of knowledge
- Poor communication skills

Appearance

At the job fair I noticed that some of the students were dressed for the interview and some were not. Students who were not dressed properly for interviewing were in their college gear and did not anticipate being offered a job. Therefore, they saw no need to wear a tie or a dress.

Many students today learn the essence and the importance of proper dressing for an interview. They learn it by chance or from reading a book. Most college campuses have a career center that is set up to not only help students find jobs, but also to help them prepare for the interview. Career centers or job placement centers have well-informed staff personnel to teach proper etiquette and interview skills. The problem is that most students never use the career centers. If you are in college, visit your campus career job placement center. It will only help you land a job.

Lack of interest

In speaking with recruiters about the "lack of interest" statement in the survey, the recruiters said that the students show little interest in what the recruiter had to say. Students did not engage in conversation or ask any questions. If you are really interested in working for a corporation, you should listen carefully and have a few prepared questions for the recruiter. You might ask the question that gets you an interview which leads to a position with that company.

Comunication skills

Moving from lack of interest to lack of knowledge on the survey, it was clear that a recruiter expects you to have some knowledge about the company.

If you are interested in a company, you should take time to do research (as mentioned earlier), and know what that company sells, their competition, mission statement, name of president, locations, etc. Your knowledge about the company shows interest and will impress the recruiter.

Communication skills today are extremely important and held in very high regard in reference to company culture. Companies are becoming more universally challenged today. They are multi-cultural, employing immigrants from all over the world. They are also trying to compete in other countries by sending their American employees overseas in an effort to expand their services. How do we understand one other? We communicate by various means such as talking, writing, body language, and facial expressions.

English is the main language in America. However, with the different cultures here, English is not always spoken with the same correctness. Sure, we are all taught English the same way in school, but some cultures have their own way of saying things. That is not all. Many times, no matter what culture a person belongs to, incorrect English—whether spoken or written—might label that person as uneducated or unsophisticated. For example, which sentence is correct?

a. That was a conversation between him and I.
b. That was a conversation between he and I.
c. That was a conversation between him and me.
d. That was a conversation between he and me.

I have heard a sentence like this one misspoken many a time, even on television. Sometimes it matters and sometimes mistakes in grammar will be missed or overlooked. My advice is to use proper grammar at all times. It is better to appear educated than not. (The answer to the above is c.)

Whether or not you speak with an accent, proper English when spoken or written is a plus. It increases your marketability to companies looking to hire you. Remember, a company's image is important and you will be promoting their image.

The other side of the survey questions was from a positive viewpoint:

What impresses you most about candidates?

These are the recruiters' answers:

   … is well dressed
   … smiles, has a good attitude
   … has good communication skills
   … is well prepared

As you can see, these aspects, which we discussed earlier, are important to recruiters. If you have ever been on an interview and you did not get the job, maybe you were not smiling. For your next interview, dress well, have a good attitude, use proper English, and prepare.

Negative attitudes are always harmful in an interview. Do not criticize your former employers. If you cannot say nice or neutral things about past jobs, it is best to say nothing if possible. For example, if the interviewer asks you how you got along with your boss at your last job and you say she was hard to get along with, she was too bossy, with a bad attitude, the recruiter may think you are the one with the bad attitude. Instead, you may want to say that Mrs. Smith was a very strict and disciplined boss, and that she was well suited for her position.

Poor appearance, showing up late, not having questions for the interviewer, improper etiquette (such as an inappropriate handshake), can all be considered mistakes during an interview. A wimpy handshake says you are not confident in yourself. A bone-crushing handshake might signal a potentially aggressive person. Let your handshake be firm, but warm.

Preparation is the key. The better prepared you are, the better you will do in the interview.

Chapter 4 :
The Interview Game

The human resource department wants to know about you and what you can tell them that is not on your resume.

Do not be surprised if you get a call from an interviewer and they ask you if you have a few minutes. The next few minutes can make you or break you, so be prepared to interview. Know what you want to say and ask. Always be ready. Keep pen and paper handy. If you are not ready to interview, tell the person that this is not the best time. Politely tell them that you were in the middle of something, and ask if you might call them back, or if they could call you back. Suggest a better time, even as short as 30 minutes later. This technique will give you time to prepare.

Interviewers ask many different questions. The most common ones, and suggested responses, follow.

Expect this question or request in every interview: **Tell me about yourself.**

This question serves several purposes: to see what your verbal communication skills are like, to learn things that may not be disclosed on your application or resume, and to break the ice and ease the interview butterflies. However, that question usually does not ease tension for you, just for the interviewer. The interviewer can sit and listen with his arms crossed as you try to talk about yourself while not appearing to be arrogant.

Answers to interview questions are easier if you are ready with good answers. So to make your answers smooth and cause you less tension, prepare canned answers that you have practiced. Start with a few lines from your resume, such as your hometown, personal interests, community involvement, and hobbies. Make sure you include why you know you are qualified for this position. This may be the only chance you get to do so.

Try to anticipate what questions will be asked, and prepare answers. Write the answers on a notepad, which you can take to the interview and refer to if necessary. Practice your interview techniques at home with a friend.

Another standard question to expect at an interview is: **Why should we hire you?**

And it's one for which you must have a good answer. Now that you know to expect this question, you can develop an answer in advance of each interview.

The basic ingredients of your answer should be universal, that is, fitting for any company. However, your answer should be tailored to fit the answer for the industry or the position for which you are applying. Your basic answer should include your having the ability to do the job, whether you are applying for a secretarial position or a plant operator. You can state why you have the ability—maybe because you have the training, education, or experience.

This is your opportunity to sell yourself on how dependable you are and will be. Explain that you have never been late or missed a day of work—but only if that is the truth. If your attendance and on-time record are not quite so spotless, explain the reasons—for instance, you are a single parent with children who are sometimes sick, or had babysitters who were not very reliable—and what steps you have taken to improve these circumstances. Say positive things as to why the company should hire you. Tell them how trustworthy you are and how part of your job is to protect the company's interests.

Corporations, as mentioned earlier, want candidates who are self-motivated. Give them some examples of circumstances that showed your initiative for a task at school, work, or community.

Other possible questions or scenarios you may be asked about include:

1. What does success mean to you?

2. Tell me about a job or task that showed you were successful.

3. Tell me about a time that there was conflict and how you handled it on the job. (If you have never had conflict on the job, think of a time of conflict you handled at school or at an organization.)

4. Tell me about your last employer and why you left. (Tip—do not be negative)

5. Why do you want to work here?

6. What do you do in your spare time?

7. Do you do any volunteer work?

8. What was your favorite boss like? And your worst boss?

9. Would you report an employee who you knew was stealing from the company?

10. What was the name of the last book you read? What was it about?

11. How would you react to being fired?

Even if you are not asked all these questions in your interview, it would be wise to have answers to as many as possible. Try not to let your responses sound rehearsed, but natural. Think about how you are going to answer each particular question before the interview. Even then, you might be asked something you were not prepared for, and may have to improvise.

When improvising, keep this suggestion in mind:

Use the first three letters of success (s-u-c) as an acronym, and pick a phrase to help you define an answer.

S tay focused

U nderstand how and where you want to go

C ommitted until the job, or interview, is finished

These techniques will help take the pressure off almost any interview.

When you answer a question, be prepared to give an example to show that you are on your toes.

Why didn't they hire me?

Keep in mind that when you interview, there are two points of view that are important: yours and the company's. When a person is not hired for a position, there would have had to be a reason, which is known as a barrier. Sometimes barriers are obvious and sometimes not. If you believe there is a barrier, you should deal with it in a positive manner to remove it from the mind of the interviewer. For example, your resume shows you have had three different employers within the past year. This could be a problem for an employer who is looking to hire a person long-term. If your interviewer does not bring it up, you should. Maybe say something like, "If you will notice on my resume, Mr. Jenkins, you will see that I have had three jobs within the past year. The reason for that is they were all temporary positions. My husband was being transferred a lot with his company; therefore I only took temporary jobs for that reason. But now he expects to be stationed here for years to come. If I should get this job, I want to make it a permanent position. I look forward to being able to retire from my next employer."

As a candidate for a position, maybe you feel inferior or doubtful that a company will hire you. A lady named Patricia applied for an engineering position in a department where all the employees were men. She had a false barrier in her mind and needed to deal with it. How did she do it? Boldly. She asked a quality question and got a quality answer. She asked the interviewer, "Mr. Harris, in the position for which you are looking to fill, do you have a preference of male or female? I have not seen any females on this floor." I do not know if that question got her the job, but of the four females interviewing for that job, she was the one who was hired. Barriers come in all sizes, some real and some only in the minds of the company and the prospect. Do not let any barriers stand in your way. Remove them with a good answer or a good question.

If there is some dark area in your past (for instance, trouble with the law or abuse of drugs) which would definitely be a barrier, it might be better to be upfront about this rather than trying to hide it. Be honest about your past weakness and what you have done to overcome your difficulties. Such honesty demonstrates your desire to improve yourself and shows a potential employer the newer, honest side of your personality. It is far better to be upfront than to have an employer find out something later that might be grounds for firing you.

The interviewer's scorecard

Each applicant is graded on several criteria, which may be different from company to company. Your interviewer might have a scorecard grading you on different categories in the interview.

The scorecard might look like this (*each attribute would get a grade, A being excellent and F being very bad*):

Coachable	(A)	B	C	D	F
Team player	A	B	C	(D)	F
Communication skills	A	B	(C)	D	F
Appearance	A	(B)	C	D	F
Attitude	A	B	C	D	(F)

It is not an easy task for a company to figure out what kind of person it is investing its valuable dollars in for training, benefits, salaries, and other cost items. This is why it is so important for companies to scrutinize candidates closely. If a candidate is coachable, she is trainable in the procedures, policies, and principles of the company. Will the candidate be open to change? Will she listen? Is she flexible?

A team player is a person who:

- Easily cooperates with other team members.
- Carries her weight on all projects.
- Is open-minded to the ideas of others and will not criticize.
- Stays on task to complete a job or mission in conjunction with other workers.

Communication is the key.

If you can communicate, you are ahead of the game. If you have poor communication skills, costly mistakes can be made. If you meant to say "She sold the car," but your team member thought you said "He stole the car," that could be a problem. Team players must always be on the same page.

Appearance is connected to image and first impressions.

How the candidate looks is a reflection on the company's image. A sloppy-looking employee can give the perception that a company is sloppy.

Employees with good attitudes

- Are easier to coach, and make better team players.
- Bring positive energy.
- Can be contagious.

Likewise, negative attitudes are also contagious. Companies do not want people with negative attitudes.

What grade would you give yourself in each category if you were the recruiter? Would you give yourself all *As*, or a combination of several grades? Ask yourself before each interview: would I hire me for that position?

If you find the question "Why should we hire you?" difficult to answer, do this. Make up an acronym to help you remember key words to your good answer. You want to focus on your qualities:

M... Motivated to do a good job

A... Attitude is positive

D... Dependable on for attendance and time-sensitive projects

F... Flexible (especially important in teaching careers)

I... Intelligent

N...Nurturing (this is also important in teaching careers)

E... Experienced

W...Willing to learn new skills

I... Intelligent

D...Dependable

E... Experienced

R... Resourceful

E... Experienced

A... Attitude is good

D...Dependable

If these suggestions don't seem quite right for you, make a list of the qualities you see in yourself and form your own acronym from the first letters in each word. If you cannot remember the acronym, write it on the notepad you will be taking to the interview.

Other questions that you might be asked are:

1. What are your greatest assets?

2. What are your weaknesses?

3. Do you like working alone or with others?

4. What did you dislike about your former employer or boss?

5. What are your goals for five years from now?

Answers (examples):

1. One of my greatest assets, as I have been told by my past supervisors, is that I always work to complete my projects on time.

2. A weakness I have is that I sometimes overwork a job, meaning that even though the job is complete, I continue trying to make it better instead of working on a new project. However, I am working on that aspect of my duties.

3. Both. I work well alone, but always see the value of teamwork on projects.

4. *Note that this question is also a negative one that requires a positive twist. You should compliment your former company and/or the boss because if you bad-mouth your old company, it is an indication that you will do the same to your new employer, plus it is unprofessional to do so. Say something like this:*

   XYZ company was a good company to work for; however, they changed bosses so fast that I could not get a handle on my jobs and goals.

Or, I had a nice boss. In fact she was too nice to her staff. It got to the point that some of the employees took advantage of her and began to slack off on their assignments, causing others to overwork in other departments.

5. I always try to set goals for myself with the company that hires me. However, at this point, I cannot set any goals until I am on the job for at least 30 to 60 days. By that time I should be able to assess what my job is and how long it will take me to master it. Then I can sit with my supervisor to set some short-term and long-term goals.

Have questions for the interviewer as well. One of the reasons why candidates do not get positions is that they do not show a strong enough interest in the company or position. When you ask questions, you are showing an interest. Recruiters expect you to ask questions. It is recommended that you do research on the company and the position and ask questions.

Here are some sample questions:

1. What challenges can I expect in this position if I am hired?

2. What are you looking for in the person you hire?

3. If I should get this position, when will I start?

4. How long is the training program for this position, if there is one?

5. Why do most employees like working for this company?

It is important not to ask about pay or benefits at this point in the interview. It might look inappropriate or unprofessional. The answers will come in plenty of time for you to make a decision if you get an offer. Also, during your research, the pay for this position should have presented itself.

Sometimes positions are plentiful, with a few qualified candidates to fill them. Other times there are plenty of candidates for the positions. Companies spend many dollars and lots of time trying to find the best person for the job. Companies want to know why they should hire you, and if you have the best answer, chances are you will get the job.

A picture speaks loudly. During your interview, be sure you are dressed in a way that reflects an impressive image the company would hire. The packaging of a present is not everything, but it helps to set the stage for what is to come. There is nothing you can say about the way you are dressed, so let your attire speak for you. Dress to impress.

It's time.

Now that you know what to say and how to look, there are a few more concerns that need to be addressed. A person who is late to an interview or an appointment might be deemed undependable, which is not a good start for a new candidate. Being late for your interview is a NO-NO. You should take every precaution to be at least 15 minutes early. If you have to, call to make sure of the location, use the Internet (MapQuest), or do a trial run the day before. Do not be late. Arriving 15 minutes early will give you time to do a final check on your appearance, and will also be a sign of dependability.

Chapter 5 :

What Your Body Language Says About You

Body language is communicating to others without using words. We communicate every day with our bodies. Our face communicates. Our hands help us to get our point across. Our body language reveals our moods.

In an interview, we must be aware of the messages we are communicating to the interviewer. From the minute you enter the room for your interview, you are sending messages. The way you walk, shake hands, sit in a chair, or your movements in your chair all say something to the interviewer.

Do you walk with confidence into the office or do you have nervous, indecisive steps? When you shake hands, are your palms sweaty? Do you have a "dead fish" handshake or a bone-crushing grip? Stand tall, take graceful steps. Dry your hands before entering the room and try gripping the interviewer's hand with the same pressure that you apply to your handshake.

When you sit after you have been invited to do so, do you slouch or sit upright? Do you have repetitive body motions, such as wringing your hands or twirling your hair with your fingers for no particular reason? Hand gestures are important, but should be used with a purpose. In Toastmasters International speaking clubs, one of the most coveted training grounds for speakers, great stress is placed on the importance of gestures in communicating on stage. Gestures help to make your voice clearer and also to more strongly make your point. However, use hand gestures to help your listener understand what you are communicating only to the degree that you want to be understood. Keep in mind that always talking with your hands can be distracting.

What is your posture while sitting? Do you cross your arms on your chest, which shows a defensive or bored mood?

Most of us are unaware of the signs we send out with our bodies. Some of these things may be positive, but others may project a negative image when we apply for a job. The best way to find out what you do that may be irritating or offensive to others is to ask your best friend. Although friends tolerate things about us that others might not, really good friends will be honest about such habits without causing hurt feelings.

What do these expressions say to you?

This position, hands crossed over the chest, might say to your interviewer, "I really don't want to be here. I am bored. I am not interested in what you have to say." The arms crossed, with fists closed, might portray a hint of aggression. If, in reality, your hands are cold, and you are ready to start shivering, speak up—"I'm sorry, it seems a bit chilly in here."

This expression and hand position speak an affirmative "I'm listening," and, "Now, what may I do for you?"

An interviewer seeing this from a potential employee is hearing, "That's an interesting idea. I could really use that in my next project."

With a look like this shouting, "Oh, Gawd, why can't my cell phone ring or something, to get me out of here!" your discomfort is clear. Don't worry, you'll be shown the door very shortly.

Chapter 6 :
If You Want a Job Done Right, Hire a Woman

Women are said to be better communicators and better dressers than men. Even though women might be more prepared and sometimes more qualified than men, women have to be more prepared in order to get the same position as a man. Yes, that did sound presumptuous. I have no scientific proof for the previous statements. They are my opinions, based on what I have observed.

In recent years, it has been debated whether a woman makes a better worker, manager, leader, or employee than a man. Of course, customs vary from one country to another. There are places in the world where women cannot test their skills, minds, and talents. In America, women have been moving up the chain of command for years.

Why hire a woman? Is a woman a better worker than a man, all things being equal? What do we mean by "all things being equal"?

Men are naturally physically stronger than women. Taking physical strength out of the equation should make things even. Let us devise a chart to judge which gender is the better risk to hire.

	Women	Men	Same
Ability			
More thorough			✓
Neatness	✓		
Attitude			
Positive outlook		✓	
Coachable	✓		
Follow company policy	✓		
Sense of humor		✓	
Dependability			
On time	✓		
Work history	✓		
Zero days missed		✓	
Trustworthiness			
Honesty	✓		
Ethics	✓		
Appearance			
Well-dressed	✓		
Company image	✓		

Of course the chart can be challenged by anyone. You could make an entirely different chart with different criteria. So, who makes a better employee, a man or a woman? This question will probably be debated for years with no clear front-runner emerging.

Women have made great strides in the workplace, especially in the years since World War II. Before that, the work place was dominated by men. Women took care of the home and family. They had the babies, took care of the babies, cleaned house, cooked, and were there for dad when he came home. How were women able to close the gender gap in job placement? When WWII hit, many men went to war, leaving many jobs to be filled. The women of America had to step up and fill the boots of those men. I am sure that other countries experienced the same circumstances. The women rolled up their sleeves and went to work outside the home as never before. Not only did they work, they also continued to have the babies, take care of the babies, clean house, and cook. If you asked most women in America today, they would say that not much has changed since WWII. Women do have abilities.

Are women positive thinkers? Are they more open-minded and less confrontational than men? Who make better listeners, men or women? Everyone knows there is a difference between men and women, but is there any difference in their attitudes at work? I once heard it said that men make company policies and women follow them. In our research, we could not discover proof that women have better attitudes than men. But if you consider which gender is more willing to cooperate, which gender follows policies more often, and which gender is more coachable, you might find that women will be your number one choice. You make the call.

If a company can hire dependable candidates, it can be sure to build a strong institution for making money. What makes an employee dependable? An employee who is punctual and completes assigned tasks on time is considered dependable. One who has limited absenteeism would be dependable. A trustworthy person would also be denoted as a dependable employee and an asset. Employees who steal from the company are liabilities no matter how well they do their job. The argument might be made that men are more dependable because, for the most part, they are not the ones who stay home with sick children, wait for the repairman, and so on, but in the twenty-first century, with so many more two-income families and single parents who are mostly mothers, this is no longer valid.

The trustworthiness of a person is vital to a company. This is why background checks today are worth the time and effort to a corporation. Employees who are not honest on their applications or resumes will probably lie in other job-related situations. Deceit discovered in background checks has eliminated many candidates from landing jobs. Theft in a company can drive it to bankruptcy. Employee theft is a bigger problem than outside shoplifters. Do you remember Enron? Employees lost jobs and pensions; customers lost money; investors, many of them senior citizens, lost their retirement savings, all because some employees were not trustworthy. The majority of those responsible for Enron's fall were men.

Employees make up a corporation. Workers who have the ability to do the job play a big part in a company's growth. When those employees are dependable, have a good attitude, and are trustworthy, the corporation can stay in business and produce products and services so it can hire you to carry on its traditions.

The endurance of women has been tested for many years. In the workplace, women have been discriminated against because of gender, but they are changing the way corporations see them. Of course, it is open to argument whether or not women are treated fairly in the workplace. One might say that women don't have as much education as men, or that they spend more time at home mothering children, and that is why they do not measure up to their male counterparts. Because women have had to fight against this type of discrimination, they are more likely to work harder simply to prove that they have what it takes.

Times are changing and it is the women who are changing things. In 1998, **Working Women: Opposing Viewpoints** published the fact that in 1960 women earned 59 cents to every dollar made by men. By 1995 women's earnings had risen to 74 cents. *Ms.* magazine stated in an article published online in 2005 that the number of women earning bachelor's degrees had reached 57.4 percent, compared to 42.6 percent for men. It was stated that this was a complete reversal of numbers recorded in 1970. However, women were still behind in numbers in Ivy League colleges and in universities that specialize in engineering or physical sciences. When some officials noted that more women were enrolling in college than men, certain colleges took a step backward to change admission requirements for men so as to try to regain parity. *Ms.* magazine noted that no one had seemed concerned when there were more men in college.[1]

Working Women: Opposing Viewpoints also noted in the 1992 census study on education that on average men worked more hours than women did. Some might contend that therefore women should be paid less, and promoted less frequently. Regardless of any reasons why women have been paid less for the same job, or not promoted at the same rate as men, women have made huge steps in the women's movement to level the playing field in corporate America.

In trying to state the reasons why women have increased their numbers in attending and graduating from college, some critics have actually tried to claim that boys are now "behind the eight ball" in elementary school, where learning techniques supposedly favor young girls. These same critics forget that elementary school teachers have predominantly been women since the end of the Civil War. If boys are at this supposed disadvantage now, why weren't women gaining in the job market and education goals until the last

1. *Ms.* magazine, http://www.msmagazine.com/fall2005/college.asp

half-century? As *Ms.* magazine aptly stated, "Maybe it's just time to let men try to catch up to us, for a change."[2]

Affirmative action was put in place for the benefit of minorities, i.e., to help equalize opportunities in the workplace by addressing inequalities in opportunities for minorities. This spilled over to benefit women as well, since they were a "minority" in most fields of work.

Women have been starting businesses for a long time. However, sometimes the "good old boy" buddy system has hampered opportunities for women in business. Since men have traditionally been at the top of the food chain in business, women have found some difficulty in creating new clients in a man's world. If a woman owned a business in the construction field, that woman might find it difficult to secure a loan to expand her business. However, if her brother with the same construction company wanted to secure a loan to expand, the doors would probably open a lot more easily. On the other hand, if a woman owned a ladies' hat store, a banker might be more open to giving her a loan. But at the same time, her brother would probably still be given the same, if not an even better, opportunity to expand that hat store. Affirmative action should make the playing field more level for women.

Take a look at how career possibilities for women have increased over the last 40 to 50 years. A woman graduating from high school in the 1960s had

2. Ibid.

about six career choices: teacher, secretary, airline stewardess (that's what flight attendants were called back then), beautician, nurse, or retail sales clerk. Many women only went to college to get their "Mrs." Degree. Nowadays, women can enter any field they choose. The glass ceiling is becoming a thing of the past, and now not even the sky is the limit. In 1983, Sally Ride was the first female American astronaut in space. Since then, many women have followed in her footsteps, and at least one woman has commanded the space shuttle.

During the Civil War, WWI, and WWII, women played a vital role in wartime efforts. They were nurses, administrative soldiers, or even pilots in the Armed Forces. Today, women are almost equal with men in the fight to keep our country safe during wartime and peace.

Women are aboard ships, flying fighter aircraft, driving tanks, and fighting on the ground as well. There has been much debate over whether women should be limited to certain duties in the Armed Forces. Some claim that women cannot perform the duties as well as men. My question is: can all men perform duties the same? I do not think so. Women have fought for equal rights for many years, and they are still fighting.

Who is stepping up to the challenge of going to school, working, raising our kids, and fighting for equality?

Women.

In today's world, multitasking is a special talent, and women are best at it. The rate of women going to school to better themselves has been increasing over the years. Women realize they cannot depend on the earnings of a man. Single moms have to do it all. Completing a degree plan may take them longer with work, school, and mothering, but women are determined not to be denied.

Remember that more women than men are now attending college and earning degrees. Statistics also show that women apply for and receive more financial aid than men. This may be due to the fact that more qualify because they are single women supporting children. Studies show that among minorities, the percentage of difference between men and women trying to better themselves with more education is even greater, with women out in front.

Women are learning the importance of education with respect to getting ahead. Women are going to school while working part-time or full-time jobs. They have multitasking down to an art. And when you add mothering to the equation, women are the best. Ask any single mom what it is like to juggle school and work while meeting the needs of a four-year-old every day. She will probably tell you it is not easy, but that she has found a way.

What some women think about the abilities of women and their importance in the workplace today:

As a director at Deloitte Tax LLP, I am active in our Women Initiative, or WIN program. Women comprise more than 50% of America's workforce. If a company does not embrace women in its workforce, it is clearly limiting its potential for growth and success. Futhermore, many companies already have women serving in high-level decision-making roles. If a company does not foster the retention and development of its women, it may miss opportunities to work with potential clients, who are looking for and expecting diversity in business. Many women excel in networking skills. Women tend to build a network of strong, long-lasting relationships with their colleagues and clients. It is this network that often brings repeated success in business.

Karen G. Blake, director, Deloitte Tax LLP

Women are champions when it comes to multitasking!
Women are designed to withstand pain easier than men.

Cynthia St. Dennis, global director of compensation

Women are terrific at multitasking, and I have yet to see a man who could even do it, much less do it well. For instance, I may have a list of 25 things to do in a day, but my husband felt he was overloaded if he had to run by the bank in addition to his normal routine, which was getting up, eating, and going to a job.

Rita Mills, publisher, New Era Times *and ABC's Press*

Some say women are too emotional to make great decisions in the business place. Well, I challenge that by saying that, because women can be emotional, we are able to make decisions from different points of view. Just because one expresses emotion doesn't necessarily mean their emotion is negative. Emotion can be positive when expressed in a constructive manner.

Kim S. Williams, airline systems specialist

A woman is thorough with the ability to accurately troubleshoot problems. A woman does not put off for tomorrow what she can do today. She is wise.

Carolyn McBride Davis, director, Career Planning and Resources,
Houston Community College Southwest

Women tend to take a more balanced view of life and add creativity to the workplace.

David Dewhurst, business owner

My experience in the business world has proven over and over that women seem to instinctively have the knack of identifying people's true motives, even when that person is trying to show otherwise. "Women's intuition" is sometimes viewed as a trite expression—but I believe it is a valuable asset in the professional world.

Vickie Staff, advertising director, My Table *magazine*

The assessment made by these women on women's ability to do a job shows the confidence of the female gender. Multitasking, emotional intuition, desire for accomplishment, and decision-making abilities are talents that seem to be in women. Women are not the only ones to praise the work of women. Below are several quotes from a male point of view over the centuries, and in today's world:

"A sufficient measure of civilization is the influence of good women."

Ralph Waldo Emerson in Society and Solitude, *1870*

"Women are not entirely wrong when they reject the rules of life prescribed for the world, for these were established by men only, without their consent."

Michel Eyquem de Montaigne in Essays, *Book III, 1588*

I feel that men and women each have unique characteristics with which they were designed. Each one's strengths were made to complement the weaknesses of the other. Since women have entered the workforce, I feel there has been a dramatic shift for the better. Where men can be bullheaded and aggressive, women are more thoughtful and cautious. Men make decisions based on fact and reason; women will rely a bit more on intuition and feeling. Each sex tends to fall on the opposite end of a spectrum. Making decisions from one end or the other can lead to abnormally great successes, but it can lead to great failures as well. Men and women working together allows businesses to consider all sides of the issue and make more informed decisions which can ensure moderate and consistent success, and lessen or eliminate failures. I have really said this over the years: hire a mom. They will finish what they need to do in time to pick up the kids at daycare. Men seem to take the same project list, work until 7 in the evening and then actually feel valued because they worked late.

Claude Thorp, Atlantis E&P Services Inc., a Hamilton Group Company

Anonymous:

"A woman's work is never done—by a man."

"God took one look at Adam and brought out a new design—Eve."

"Women's rights became a movement...because of man's wrongs."

Good Is Not Enough: And Other Unwritten Rules for Minority Professionals, a well-written and very informative book for minority professionals by Keith R. Wyche with Sonia Alleyne, echoes what the women above have said: that women are more intuitive. They are better forecasters. They have abilities that are many times discounted, like their instinct to adjust to the situation. Women are more caring about other people; this makes them nurturing and insightful about the needs of employees. Also, as we have already said, females are better communicators in that they are champions at expressing themselves. Added to that, they make good listeners, which is necessary for solving problems.

On page 164 of **Good Is Not Enough**, the authors refer to some other books, including **Pitch Like a Girl: How a Woman Can Be Herself and Still Succeed**, by Ronna Lichtenberg (Rodale, 2005), where the author breaks down the different management styles by gender. He talks about how women use part of their brain to process information to multitask, where men do not. Women are good negotiators. They think more about the outcome, which results in a win—win situation for both sides.

Chapter 7 :
What Makes A Woman
A Woman?

Words describe everything we know and feel. What we feel is sometimes hard to capture with words, but some words have special significance:

Word: a speech sound, or series of such sounds, having meaning as a unit of language.

Values: the ideals and goodness in a person; judgement of morals and doing the right thing.

Character: qualities of courage, honesty, and integrity.

Honesty: freedom from deceit or fraud.

Integrity: adherence to ethical principles; soundness of moral character; honesty.

The words above, and others like them, are often used to describe businesswomen.

You might be saying, not all businesswomen have those characteristics. What about Martha Stewart? She went to prison for fraud. In my opinion, the fact that one woman went to prison does not make all women guilty. Or to twist a cliché, one bad apple doesn't spoil the whole barrel. There are many people in jail who are taking the fall for someone else. Maybe Ms. Stewart was innocent. Maybe someone else was the leader of this fraud, and Ms. Stewart, as owner of the company, was held responsible for the crime. Because of her integrity, she did the time. And, if she was truly guilty, she took the responsibility for what she did, rather than passing the buck.

Other words associated with women are:

Loyalty: the state or quality of being loyal; faithfulness to commitments or obligations.

Intuitive: being able to perceive the truth about a situation or a person, or having the insight to form a conclusion without rational thought.

Carol Latham, in Margaret Heffernan's book **Women on Top**, had intuition. She was able to make the right move at the right time in the market. She started a successful business when no one else around her thought it would work. They could not see what her instincts were telling her.[1]

1. Margaret Heffernan, **Woman on Top** (New York: Penguin Books, 2008), 17.

Nurture: to support and encourage, as during a period of training or development.

Empathy: understanding, being aware of, or sensitive to, the feelings and thoughts of others.

"Empathy" is an abstract word that you cannot describe in a physical sense. It is a word that is best defined by action. Cindy, an employee of Ties Required for only three months, had taken sick. The office manager, Lucy, offered her two of her sick days. Three other ladies also chipped in with a day each, giving Cindy a week of sick leave. If the women had not understood the condition that Cindy was in, she would have had to quit and go on welfare. Stories of women's empathy and their ability to nurture people abound in the fields of education and medicine.

Cooperative: possessing a willingness and ability to work with others.

A man started his new business, a hardware store on Main Street. His business was projected to do well in the town of Beaumont. Another man opened a plumbing store next door. Both were doing very well initially. But both men were very ambitious and competitive. Each owner wanted to grow his business, but the market would only support the volume of business they currently had. So, the hardware store owner began to carry plumbing products. This made the plumbing store owner angry, so he started to carry a line of hardware goods. Each owner kept adding to their lines and trying to outdo the other. They began price wars. Each man believed that if he could run the other one out of business, he could have it all to himself. Eventually, after all the wars and competitive dealings, both stores went out of business.

A woman opened a donut shop on Main Street in the vacant hardware store, where she sold donuts, kolaches, pastries, and coffee. Another woman opened a sandwich and soft drink shop in the old plumbing store. Both women wanted to grow their businesses. Because women are great communicators, very smart, and very cooperative, the two women came to an agreement. They decided to form a partnership to expand their businesses, and now have a catering business that serves a bigger market than expected.

Philanthropist: one who dispenses aid from funds set aside for humanitarian purposes, or one who contributes funds and/or time to such causes.

Women in business give back to the community proportionately far more than do other businesses.

Women respect values. Values "are what people work *for*, the thing beyond cash remuneration that gives their work meaning and purpose."[2]

2. Ibid., 51.

Where do women get their fight? Women have been fighting for equality for years. They have fought for equal rights in sports, education, politics, and in corporate America. Will things ever be equal? Who knows? Many women in the mainstream workplace have gotten fed up with fighting for equal rights, or are too busy working nowadays.

In **Women on Top**, Margaret Heffernan reports that 40 percent of US firms are owned or controlled by women.[3] For a long time, women have been overlooked for their talents, but now many of them have built on their skills and started their own businesses. Women just like you have many dynamic abilities, are willing to go for it, and do.

Sometimes tough economic conditions will create opportunities for risk takers and many women are taking some risk.

Heffernan talks about a multitude of women who went from corporate life to entrepreneurship. Some of these women were laid off from their jobs and needed to create opportunities. Some were smart enough to see the trends of the future and seized the moment to start their businesses. Heffernan also talks about women who borrowed money from friends to start their business and developed very profitable companies. Some of the women she writes about were officers of large firms in which they did not get the respect they deserved.

3. Ibid., ix.

This unfair treatment pushed them to start their own businesses. Brenda Rivers, founder of Andavo Travels, a $100 million business, says women have had it tough, but they made it anyway. Rivers has other businesses as well.

For a variety of reasons, today there are more successful women entrepreneurs than ever before. What is clear from Heffernan's book is that a woman will succeed at whatever she does if she believes in herself.

Conclusion

Through these chapters we have seen that women can and do excel in every area of life and in the workplace. They talk. They act. In other words, they talk the talk and they walk the walk. They do this at every level of business and in every type of career. Because they are resourceful, intuitive, empathetic, and possess other important values, there are some areas in which they are outdoing men.

Today, women of all ages can join their sisters and become successful in whatever they endeavor to do. They need only follow the steps lined out for them by their successful sisters:

Seek what your heart tells you to do. Imagine your dream job. Match it with your personality and individual skills.

Search for the company best suited to your abilities and dreams. Apply to that and similar companies.

Dress for success. Remember that conservative business attire will make the best impression.

Prepare for your interview. Communicate your ambitions and abilities with your words and your body language.

Do not be afraid to change careers when family circumstances change or when job burnout rears its ugly head.

Do not be afraid to take risks and strike out with a business of your own.

Remember the many virtues women have which make them more special, and in many cases better qualified, than men.

Become the best woman you can be in your chosen career.

Appendix

Women will find other useful resources in the books, Web sites and organizations listed below:

Sites you should Google:

www.dressforsuccess.org

www.allbusiness.com

http://usadollargrants.com/womengrants.html

www.dik.gov/dol/audience/aud-women.htm

www.usagrantapplications.org

www.wbsnon.org
Women's Business Support Network Foundation, Inc.
PO Box 572563
Houston, Texas 77257-2563

www.nafe.com
National Association for Female Executives

Women's Sizes

Women's Dresses (Misses Sizes)

USA	4	6	8	10	12	14	16	18
Europe	34	36	38	40	42	44	46	48
UK	6	8	10	12	14	16	18	20
Japan	3	5	7	9	11	13	15	17

Women's Dresses (Junior Sizes)

USA	3	5	7	9	11	13	15
Europe	30	32	34	36	38	40	42
UK	5	7	9	11	13	15	17
Japan	2	4	6	8	10	12	14

Women's Dresses (Women's Sizes)

USA	32	34	36	38	40	42	44	46
Europe	42	44	46	48	50	52	54	56
UK	34	36	38	40	42	44	46	48
Japan	31	33	35	37	39	41	43	45

Women's Blouses and Sweaters

USA	32	34	36	38	40	42	44	46
Europe	38	40	42	44	46	48	50	52

Women's Shoes

USA	4	5	6	7	8	9	10
Europe	36	37	38	39	40	41	42
UK	$2\frac{1}{2}$	$3\frac{1}{2}$	$4\frac{1}{2}$	$5\frac{1}{2}$	$6\frac{1}{2}$	$7\frac{1}{2}$	$8\frac{1}{2}$
Japan	21	22	23	24	25	26	27

Acknowledgements

Special Thanks

Clothing
JC Penney

Publishing Consultant
Rita Mills

Book Developer
Deborah Fronteria

Graphic Design
Kristin Kearns / BurningDesignerStudios
burningdesigner@hotmail.com

Editing
Shirin Wright
proofwrite@hotmail.com

Photography
K&M Publishing, Inc., Houston, Texas

Models
Summer Adair
Jamesia King
Sarah Moomaw
Dwan Reed

Bibliography

Angel, Debra L., and Elisabeth E. Harney. **No One Is Unemployable: Creative Solutions for Overcoming Barriers to Employment**. WorkNet Training Services, 1997.

Heffernan, Margaret. **Women on Top**. New York: Penguin Books, 2008.

Rosser, Phyllis. "Too Many Women in College?" *Ms.* magazine (fall 2005), http://www.msmagazine.com/fall2005/college.asp (accessed Jan. 11, 2010).

Wyche, Keith R. **Good Is Not Enough: And Other Unwritten Rules for Minority Professionals**. With Sonia Alleyne. New York: Portfolio, Penguin Books, 2008.

About the Authors

Michael "Beau" Williams

Paris Williams

Having been in the clothing business as a retail sales manager, assistant to distribution allocators, and outside sales rep for over 20 years, Beau has advised thousands of men on how to look their best. A speaker at college campuses, he gives young men valuable tips on appropriate clothing for the all-important job interview. Born in Beaumont, Texas, Beau now lives in Houston. He is a graduate of Lamar University, with a BBA in marketing and a focus on fashion merchandising.

Paris N. Williams is a Beaumont, Texas, native now residing in St. Louis, Missouri. Paris is a student majoring in business administration. She is an entrepreneur owner of JLSM Modeling and Etiquette School that focuses on working with youth.

Index